FINDING THE PERFECT COACH FOR YOU

Navigating the world of online coaches

Copyright © 2015 Rebecca Clark

All rights reserved. No part of this publication may be reproduced, stored in a retrieval system, or transmitted, in any form or by any means, electronic, mechanical, photocopying, recording, or otherwise, without prior written permission from the publisher or author.

ISBN Print 97-81790659524

FINDING THE PERFECT COACH FOR YOU

Navigating the world of online coaches

BY REBECCA CLARK

DEDICATION

This book is dedicated to the coaches that freely share their expertise in our online Nudge Village community.

Barbara Christensen - Bija Health Coaching
http://www.bijacoaching.com

Robert Kennedy - RJKIII Consulting
http://www.robertkennedy3.com

Chris Miles - Money Ripples
http://www.moneyripples.com

Julie Mueller - Chicks Connect
http://www.chicksconnect.com

Tanya Smith - Tanya Smith Coaching
http://www.tanyasmithonline.com

Heidi Totten - Inspire the Sprouts
http://www.inspirethesprouts.com

TABLE OF CONTENTS

Dedication	5
Table of Contents	7
Introduction	9
Picking a Coach	13
The Factors	27
Aligned Values	29
Experience – Been There, Done That	33
Certification and Training	37
The Referral	45
Personality	51
Hold Me Accountable	55
Administrative	63
Reliable	67
Communication	69
Network and Resources	73
Product Portfolio	77
Time	81
Confidentiality - The Human Vault	89
Emotional Intelligence	91
Let's Talk Money	95
Criteria Worksheet	103
Experiment – Mistakes and Lessons	107
Outgrowing the Coach	109
Now, Go – Find the Perfect Coach for You	113
Books	115
About the Author	117

INTRODUCTION

Growth is never by mere chance;
it is the result of forces working together.
~ James Cash Penney

I need to be willing to pay for personal growth. At least that is what people seem to say each day in books, online, and at work. The groups I participate in, and network with, are filled with people that are deeply committed to personal growth and achievement. Though many resources are free, they've encouraged me to pay to get resources to support my growth. Sometimes I do. Sometimes I don't. Sometimes it works, sometimes I'm not sure, and sometimes I am sure that it doesn't help. Still, I've experienced those moments of going into autopilot in relationships, career, eating habits, and other areas of life. This is especially true if what I am doing seems to be good enough and doesn't seem to rock any boats.

After completing graduate school, I got busy applying my new-found knowledge on the job. I was soon so overwhelmed with projects and tasks and most of my time was spent leading, managing, training and mentoring others. Training and mentoring are excellent learning tools, until you are re-teaching and re-learning the same information over and over. While those you help move forward, you can find yourself stagnate and stale. I needed to take more time to grow. And, to trust that growth could come from seeking outside help.

In the book called *The E-Myth Mastery*, Michael E. Gerber points out that in order to truly commit to personal growth and become a master in our area of interest, we need outside help. I didn't edit the quote because I felt he captured what needed to be said. Gerber states,

> "In short, to achieve Mastery one must achieve Clarity. And to achieve clarity, most often requires an outside influence, someone who can pull you out of yourself so that you can more readily see yourself, someone who can challenge your assumptions, your beliefs, the habits that determine what you do in reaction to what happens to you, the opinions you hold, the walls you set up to keep your life comfortable, unthreatened, unchallenged. It is hard to see ourselves without the eyes of another. A coach, a confidant, a mentor, a teacher. She always surrounds herself with people who know more than she does, with people who are as good at what they do as she is at what she does, people who are committed to her growth and her vision, people who are inspired and inspiring, people who are so committed to engaging with life in a world class way that they never let the people who depend upon them play anything less than a world class game, people who are trustworthy and demand the same from the people they serve, people who accept nothing less than optimal results."

No doubt you've already realized the importance of looking outside yourself and that's why you picked up this book. You are on a mission to find the best coach for you. Whether you've already worked with coaches, are looking to find your first coach, want to become a coach, or are a coach seeking to better meet your client's needs, this book is for you. It is heavily focused on coaches found through online connections and websites, but the principles apply in any coaching relationship. It is intended to be a resource to re-visit along your journey of personal improvement.

PICKING A COACH

*Each person holds so much power within themselves that
needs to be let out. Sometimes they just need a little nudge,
a little direction, a little support, a little coaching,
and the greatest things can happen.*
~ Pete Carroll

How hard can it be to pick a coach?

There are thousands of online coaches depending upon your needs, preferences, and time. You have many options. There are coaches to help you lose weight or gain weight, teach how to start a business, run a business and sell a business. There are coaches that teach you how to have a better marriage, think big and grow rich, or even how to provide a better grooming experience for a precious pet. Yes. You can get coached on anything, anywhere and from anyone.

With so many options, it shouldn't be that hard to find a great coach to accomplish personal goals, grow professionally, or obtain success. Yet, it is. And, it is easy to make mistakes in your coach selections all the time and at great personal cost.

Many of us spend thousands of dollars before we realize that we might have selected the wrong coach! Though we like to trust our mental capacities, they can, and often do fail us when we make these types of decisions. I saw a posting online the other day that showed a photo of a full grocery cart and the caption read – "I went to the store for shampoo and came home with a cart full of stuff and …no shampoo."

Does this sound familiar? The nice to haves in our lives suddenly take on great importance when we enter a store (in-person or online) and see all the other options available. Tack on a special deal or limited time offer and some of our common sense just floats right out the window. It happens in online interactions with all the gorgeous websites and enticing marketing. It feels impossible to pass up opportunities presented by people that promise to change our lives, turn our business into a six-figure success with a few easy steps, and give us the life we always envisioned. I've fallen into the traps but have also learned some lessons along the way.

That's why I've written this book.

Finding the right coach to help us achieve our goals is no easy task. We are swayed by the attractive face, the glossy pictures, and a few good recommendations from the "right" people.

But, let's be honest with ourselves up front. Try as you might, you aren't going to follow all the criteria provided in this book. You may have the best of intentions, like I did, and even start a robust spreadsheet filled with carefully selected factors and criteria, complex formulae and weighted values to determine who the best coach is for you. It might look cool and pop out a few high scores for your best fit, but the reality is you'd probably disregard the sheet in favor of someone you "just have to work with."

Still, this is an attempt to at least train the brain on some factors to think about when you are in that moment of decision. Maybe some of these factors will pop into your head when your hand is screaming to touch the "Buy Now" button for that deal of a lifetime.

If you've developed the habit of referencing a set of criteria when you are making decisions, you at least have a chance of making fewer mistakes…even if a little emotion slides in.

My father shared with me a story from back in the 1980s when he was searching for a new (to us) car for the family. He created a list of requirements that he wanted in a car and used the list every time he went to check out a car. He searched and searched and finally found a car that met the requirements. However, years later he admits that it really didn't meet all the requirements. It might have been the innovative stereo system that caught his eye and really enamored him to the point of purchase.

Had he really followed his list? Yes, for the most part. But, once many of the criteria he had listed had been met, some of it took on greater importance. Apparently, the stereo system suddenly became vastly important. In my teenage mind, stereo systems were ok, but big dark green station wagons with faux leather seats were not! It was even worse when we bought the car and later my mother slid into a tree during a

Michigan ice storm. Green car plus faux leather seats and a big dent in the rear door equals not cool! Hidden under the ugly exterior there was at least …a good stereo.

Even though I know that you will go about finding a coach with the best of intentions, and armed with all the right criteria, you will likely make hasty buying decisions. At the last minute some criteria will become more important to you than others. Over time, and perhaps with a few mistakes under your belt, you'll become extremely savvy on what to look for, where to take the risks, and to modify your search to fit your needs. They key word being "Your" needs. This is a coach for you and not your friend, spouse, or co-worker.

Each experience gives you the expertise you need toward finding someone that is a better fit for you at the point of life you are in and for your coaching needs. As you maneuver the ever-changing landscape, you'll also start to quickly recognize the opportunities for true growth and the options you can let float right by. As your needs change along the way, you will outgrow some coaches and must keep stepping up your coach finding game!

Hopefully you won't have to fly across your country and drive hours out to a desolate ranch to learn your lessons. But, I did.

The Retreat

When I was in the fourth grade, I started delivering the Midland Daily News in Midland, Michigan. I was under the 12-year-old minimum age limit, but I was anxious to become a paper girl. I was tall for my age and they needed someone local for the route. They figured I looked old enough, and was willing, and I got the job! At the same time, I started babysitting for family friends and started mowing the neighbor's lawn. I was quite the entrepreneur, before I had heard of the word!

As a teenager I added making and selling chocolate suckers to my portfolio of side enterprises and even got a little crafty with silk and lace covered photo albums. They were fun endeavors and I grew, but ultimately ended up going back to hourly jobs and eventually joined the ranks of salaried employees.

I was doing well, having earned six figures as a full-time employee for 6-7 years. But, I was anxious. I wanted to become a full-time entrepreneur. I guess when you start hitting the "six figures" mark on a regular basis, you start to realize that all the studies are right. Making more doesn't make you happier; doing what you enjoy makes you happier. Of course, this assumes the essentials are met. There are a lot of studies out there that prove this, but let's keep the story going.

In my dissatisfaction, I wanted to return to a former dream – to become an entrepreneur. I figured that I needed to learn from people that had already found success in entrepreneurship. I started listening to podcasts and reading books, and ultimately realized that I needed to start paying for coaches. And, pay them I did! Internet marketing coaches, health coaches, business coaches, and product development coaches. Their online profiles, websites, and products screamed success and I was anxious to learn how to make the transition to their lifestyle. A lifestyle that didn't include 6-8 meetings a day, cube farms, conference calls, and long commutes in stifling Washington, DC traffic.

A respected friend sold me on a business retreat that would teach me some of the basics to get started. I was excited and intimidated. I'd be interacting with experts that had already *made it* in the world of entrepreneurship and would teach me how to get started. I wasn't completely uninformed. I had already learned a lot about the tools, principles and approaches of online marketing before walking in the door. I'd been a blogger since 2005 and was an early adopter of the so-called web 2.0 tools (e.g. blogs, wikis, Facebook, Twitter, anything in the cloud). But I knew there must be an actual secret formula somewhere that I was missing. I just knew that this retreat would unveil that secret to me.

I bought a plane ticket, flew across the United States, rented a car, and I drove over three hours to the middle of nowhere to a beautiful ranch. As the coaches and clients arrived it was obvious, they were a group of kind, fun people that were ready to learn all about becoming a success in business. Many of them already seemed to know each other well and so that added to the intimidation factor for those of us that weren't in their social circle. Plus, they were a far cry from the type A, black-suited, uptight, hustle-n-bustle power driven DC crowd I'd been part of for the last 15 or more years. They danced and sang during every 10-minute break (and there was no alcohol involved)!

We gathered informally on chairs, sofas and large bean bags facing a presentation screen. It was time to settle in for a series of training activities that would change our lives and our business.

Except, it didn't. Not for me. After the first morning, it was crystal clear. I was not in the target audience for this retreat. I wasn't learning anything new.

Don't get me wrong. I'm a learner. I carry a notebook and device everywhere I go in case someone says something profound or I get a big idea. I take notes at church, on the metro and even at a stoplight if something thought provoking comes up on the radio. It's just that I had already heard this before. I didn't mean I was great at all of it. By no means should I be writing taglines or marketing copy for myself or anyone else, but I did know that it was important and where to find someone to take care of it for me.

Others in the room were having life changing moments. I had undervalued my experience and education. My corporate experiences of the last 20 years were valuable in the world of entrepreneurship. What a nice surprise! I used systems, standards, processes, and budgets daily. I led dozens of diverse virtual teams toward producing large classroom and online courses. I dealt with high ranking military leaders, company presidents and other C-level officials. I settled disputes amongst team members. I managed multi-million-dollar contracts daily, and I learned through tough experience how important that the culture and internal politics play day-to-day in getting work done (or not) in large organizations.

Yet, standing before me training me were people that had experienced business success for 1-3 years in a very small niche. Most of their success was from training people in what they were successful implementing once or twice with 1-2 products. Nothing wrong with that, but no one had gone through a tough market, a lawsuit, an onslaught of bad press, or a disruptive innovation. Most of the people in the room were eating up all the information. Most of it was information that we could find on the Internet for free – then and now. Create a personal brand, set up a website, use social media tools, create a sales pipeline and set up an approach to help you execute tasks personally and in a team environment. The secret formula ended up being the equivalent of a beginning project management course. Yikes, I had over 10 years of project management and a Professional certification in Project Management. Shame on me. I had under-estimated myself and for that I was both thrilled and devastated.

I was devastated that I had spent time and money during a very busy and stressful time in my life to fly across the country to attend this retreat. In other respects, it was a huge confidence boost. I knew stuff! And what I knew was re-usable in the entrepreneurial environment in more ways than I realized. The gurus I was intimidated by were far less experienced than I was. Though they offered the exact material that many of the retreat participants needed, it wasn't enough for me. I already knew what they knew. I just needed a product to apply it to, which has proven to be my most difficult challenge. It still gave me confidence. I could do this! People might learn from me and pay me for what I knew. After all, I had paid people with less education and experience to teach me. Why couldn't I apply my skills and become a successful entrepreneur as well?

I did re-learn one concept at the retreat, and it was that hustle matters. Hard work pays off. Keep at it regardless of your privileges, education or experience. Success can come to those who work toward it. The coaches at the retreat were hustlers!

Ironically, my free time at the retreat didn't involve setting up my business as was promised because the coaches targeted me for an up-sell opportunity. It would have cost $20k+in coaching and another $5k in airplane flights over the course of the next year. Though I know this coaching package was worth every penny for the few that signed up, it wasn't wise for me and I backed out of the "yes" I squeaked out during the hard sell and went on my way. Part of this package was to work toward becoming a "national speaker." I regularly speak at large national conferences for my day job. Can I improve in this area? Yes. But, I think I can do it closer to home, with more specific tutoring and mentoring related to the career field that I'm in at this time. Plus, I know that most keynotes don't come from random picks from national speaking websites. They come from personal references or from those running in certain circles of expertise.

This retreat was a big turning point for me in my coaching activities. It isn't the only "a-ha" experience I've had working with coaches found online. But, it was the most expensive as far as time and money. I flew across the United States, rented a car and drove 3-4 hours out to an obscure ranch and back. It can't help but stand out as an instructive memory.

Do I consider it a waste? Absolutely not! This, and other experiences, taught me how to step back and take a little more time when selecting who I will take time to partner with, learn from, and aspire to be. I realized that I was not a candidate for these types of retreats. Perhaps a small group or one-on-one sessions with experienced coaches in specific areas of expertise would work better for me. And, not have to worry about sleeping in a room full of strangers.

Though discrimination isn't right in how we treat human beings in general, we do need to take time to be selective in whom we choose to learn from, receive guidance from and ultimately send our hard-earned money. On the flip side, it doesn't help the reputation of a coach to work with clients that aren't aligned to their strengths and values. With that thought in mind, a book like this is also valuable for a coach to ensure they are attuned to what they offer, how they offer it, and what clients they should seek.

Note: Are you wondering if I still listen to advice from the friend that referred me to the retreat? Yes. Yes, I do. She realized that I was the wrong target audience about the same time I did. She has referred me to many other wonderful contacts since that time.

Marketing goes a LONG way in convincing that XYZ person is the right person for YOU…and everyone else. Even the most logical people can be lured in by the professional website, the slick video presentation, and a well-crafted message.

There are so many alternatives out there right now. The ease of entering the marketplace makes it possible for undiscovered talent to rise to the top and …mediocre talent and wannabes as well.

Treat this like a job search – you are interviewing them just as much as they are interviewing you. After all, as an employee or a consultant, you are the person that must be motivated, talented, and hardworking to get the job done. You don't want to be that person that isn't the right fit, no matter how desperate you are for a paycheck. It could put a stain on your personal reputation and possibly get you fired. Either way, it is uncomfortable.

Selecting a coach requires both parties to ensure that they are the right fit for each other. Luckily, many coaches are conducting pre-screens now to find out if they are the right fit before moving forward. Any time spent on this on the front end saves a lot of pain and anxiety later. It also spares both parties the "I would like a refund" conversation. So, take advantage of those free coaching sessions that come your way. It is your chance to interview a potential coach.

If you are going to spend any money at all, why not take a little bit of time to find out if who and what you are getting fits your needs?

In my experience at the beautiful ranch, I realized that this was a life changing experience for some of the people in the room. Isn't that wonderful? They somehow met the right person at the right time. I know the feeling. I've had it before. It is life changing. It is like an entirely new door opens that you didn't know existed and you suddenly feel like you are exposed to all the possibilities and opportunities that the world has to offer.

But it wasn't the right fit for me. I knew 90% of what was shared. I had applied it for years and didn't know that it was considered rocket science in some minds.

Luckily, with all the options out there, there is one for you.

Along the same lines as one size doesn't fit all, is the realization that one coach won't fit all your personal learning, accountability or support needs.

A coach that might be great at holding you accountable to your weight goals might not know anything about helping you set up a process for dealing with personal clients in a business. A business coach might not be the person that you work with to discuss innovative ideas to implement in your next product launch, but may be awesome at helping you set up a system to run your business. A coach that helps you with your innovative ideas might not be the same person you speak with about a deeply spiritual issue.

The beauty of this is that we can select different people to assist us with different needs. Every coach doesn't have to meet all our personal criteria. They just might fit 1-2 specific criteria if you have a very specific need.

When I realized that I could have multiple health coaches, business coaches, and leadership mentors, the world opened. It was acceptable to learn by interacting with many people.

Coach Mania

As a side note, don't connect and work with too many coaches at once. It gets time consuming and confusing. At the end of the day you are working with coaches so you can perform better. Having to be accountable to multiple coaches can drive anyone into anxiety and despair over not being able to accomplish all the various goals, assignments, conference calls, and other obligations related to being mentored.

This is your chance to focus and make improvements in your life. Give yourself the gift of focusing on something small first and then add to that load as your capacity to accept more relationships, goals, and improvements increase.

Are you anxious to get to the factors to consider? The criteria that will help you find the best coach for you? I sure am! Let's get started.

THE FACTORS

*The ultimate authority must always rest with
the individual's own reason and critical analysis.*
~ Dalai Lama

After signing up for numerous coaching programs and following numerous coaches online, I've developed a list of factors (or criteria) that I use in selecting people that I work with in my personal and professional life. I'm not too rigid. No matter how many of the factors a person satisfies, there could be that little gnawing feeling that they are still the wrong person to partner with in your quest for improvement. Or, in the other direction – they are way too advanced and you aren't yet ready for that level of growth.

These factors can serve as guidelines as you look at options and make decisions. You will grow, and as you do so you may outgrow your coach!

Before Hitting the "Buy Now" Button

My friend Pamela Harrison tells me to "sleep on it" when I'm making a big decision. I highly recommend doing just that whenever making any decision involving time or money. We aren't talking about small purchases that you make every day. It is making decisions on time and money that go beyond your personal comfort zone or threshold. For some it may be

$50, and others are comfortable quickly hitting the "Pay Now" button for any items under $500. Whatever that threshold is, you know it because you've most likely experienced the anxiety that can descend upon you when there is pressure to make a wise choice.

This is the quick list of factors to consider when selecting a coach to guide you on your journey:

- Aligned Values
- Experience
- Certification and Training
- Referral
- Personality
- Accountability
- Administrative
- Reliability
- Communication
- Network and Resources
- Product Portfolio
- Time Commitment
- Confidentiality (Human Vault)
- Emotional Intelligence
- Money (cost)

So, let's dive in!

ALIGNED VALUES

*When your values are clear to you,
making decisions becomes easier.
~ Roy E. Disney*

If you are learning how to eat healthy, does it really matter if your coach attends the same church you attend, chooses the same political party or uses their spare time in the same way you do?

Maybe. Maybe not.

In the case of healthy eating, it might. Those who are living certain religious or lifestyle standards (e.g. Muslim, Hindu, The Church of Jesus Christ of Latter-Day Saints, Seventh Day Adventist, vegetarian, etc.) refrain from eating or using certain substances. A coach that doesn't subscribe to the exact limitations of these values could be a devastating choice for some of these people. It hits at the center of their values. It is a deal breaker and could be a massive waste of time and money if these aren't known up front. It's even worse if the coach doesn't respect the choices that are made.

If I'm learning a programming language on the computer, it may not matter. There are certain programming codes that must be used and have certain meaning regardless of our preferences.

Still, it may matter to you. If you want to be an ethical programmer, you certainly don't want to be learning from someone who regularly hacks into corporate or personal computers whenever they are angry about a product or service. But, what if the hacker is paid to hack for national security or to determine who is hacking into a system they manage? That may take on an entirely different meaning. You get to decide what that means to you.

The point is that we all have a certain value system and we shouldn't have to break it when we select a coach. In fact, this is the time to honor your personal value system the most.

I've gained a few lessons learned in this area. I thought it didn't matter if I learned about business and marketing from people with different values. It turns out that it matters to me. All the coaches I've worked with are ethical, kind, successful and innovative. Here and there they will infuse some of their personal lifestyle and political choices that are in direct conflict to my own. I try not to let it bother me, but deep down it sometimes does. This is especially true when I observe them making online statements and value judgments about people with certain beliefs. So, this has become a criterion that I look at when I'm working with most of my coaches. On the other hand, I don't care so much if I'm learning about web design, technology tools, etc. They must treat me and others well, share helpful insights and lead me toward better work. I'm fine with that because these are generally acceptable human behaviors.

Recently I took a chance with two coaches that I thought I might like to work with despite their swearing habits. By taking a chance, I mean that I bought their books to learn more about their approach and gain some insights. Both coaches stated a few things that truly inspired me and helped me make some better decisions, but then the intense swearing and the unnecessarily vulgar stories and language became too much for me. On the quest to become my best, good and better isn't as good as best. I'm appreciating what I learned from their books and will not be paying for their services in the future. Still, I don't mind reading their blogposts or Facebook feeds occasionally.

There are too many options out there to settle in this area. If you are looking for a personal life coach, please keep this factor at the top of your list.

Aligned Values Questions to Ponder

- What type of coaching am I seeking?
- Does that coaching rely heavily on applying principles that align with my personal value system?
- How deeply do my personal values and the coaches value align for this area of growth?
- Have I taken the time to find out more about the coach's values and background?

EXPERIENCE – BEEN THERE, DONE THAT

*A mind that is stretched by a new experience
can never go back to its old dimensions.
~ Oliver Wendell Holmes, Jr.*

The story about my experience at the ranch retreat is an example of how my skills and experience didn't match up to my expectation of a coach. For $2,500 I should have walked away with something new. Part of my brain knew this, but the marketing was so compelling and the person who referred me was so convincing that I decided to attend. I was reminded of key principles and approaches to use in setting up a business strategy, and it was neatly compiled into one notebook. It just wasn't new to me. Maybe the reason for the retreat was to share the outcome with you! If so, it was worth it.

A few years ago, I was taking a walk and listening to an Entrepreneurship podcast (a Dave Ramsey production). The interviewer was speaking to an author about his book. I still remember the moment he made this point – if you are at the top of your class, you are in the wrong class. It might not be a direct quote, but that is what I heard. All kinds of emotions came out of me when I realized that I was in that situation at work. I was so busy with so many projects that I was in a never-ending mode of helping mentor others. Yet, I needed to progress too. Otherwise, my job the rest of my life would be that of continually training whatever new government or contractor employee came through the door to create products for us. Some may be fine with that stability and familiarity with the job. I am not. I needed to keep growing and learning and expanding my horizons and capabilities. My experience and my job were now becoming a hindrance to my own progress.

Experience means a lot. It informs our decision-making and can help us assist others to avoid the mishaps and diversions that are inevitable on the path to growth.

It is worth taking a moment to find out more about the coach's experience and see if that is important to you. My professional respect for someone increases as I see a combination of years in the field they represent and accompanied by a healthy amount of innovative thought. That's important to me because I've taken the time to do that in my field and I want that from someone that coaches me. If you've been around a while, you know that experience is a combination of failures and successes that provide depth to lessons learned.

Depending upon the area of coaching, just a little more experience than yours may be enough. A coach that set up 4-5 websites might be able to easily coach you through some best practices, tips, and step-by-step approaches that worked for them. If you are expecting to make major life shifts or career changes, you need someone that has helped people in a variety of circumstances and mindsets, so they can monitor and adjust their coaching sessions with you as you collect the ideas and concerns you may have related to your goals.

Like all the factors, you get to decide how important this is for your specific need.

Experience Questions to Ponder

- Is their experience similar what you are seeking to accomplish?
- Do you respect their background experiences?
- Is their experience broad enough or focused enough for what you need to learn or the changes you need to make?
- How long have they been doing what they are doing?
- Does it matter how long they've had this experience or is it something that could be learned in a short period of time?
- Does the person referring you to them know YOUR background and experience?

CERTIFICATION AND TRAINING

> Education is that whole system of human training within and without the schoolhouse walls, which molds and develops men.
> ~ W. E. B. Du Bois

This is the perfect time to address a related factor in making your coaching selection – does the coach have certification or formal training in the area of their claimed expertise?

This isn't important to everyone. In all the recruiting efforts I've been involved in for various organizations, I have rarely seen a credential be the reason we've hired someone. It may have influenced us to select the person over another candidate with the same level of experience, but we never knowingly selected someone with a credential over someone that had more experience. Even now, I work for an organization that really does prefer master's degrees and doctorates. There are always plenty of applicants with higher degrees and certifications, but there have been times I've bypassed all of them for the person with the bachelor's degree and the right experience.

For those in the United States, you may remember a reality show dividing contestant into teams – the book smarts (contestants with MBAs) vs. the street smarts (contestants that had learned lessons from their experience) to complete weekly challenges. As each week played on, various contestants fell out of the game from both the book smarts and street smarts teams. In the end, a book smarts contestant won the final challenge. However, looking at the statistics from Wikipedia on January 9, 2015, as each week went by, there was consistently approximately the same number of contestants winning and losing from both teams.

The street smarts were called "Net Worth" because they had higher net worth than their highly educated counterparts. Education is great, but it doesn't necessarily translate into a higher net worth. Net worth may or may not be important to you, but this is humbling for those of us with advanced degrees and multiple certifications. It provides us with some information that should help us in selecting our next coach. Our experience and our education matter, no matter what forms they come in. But, they are just some of the factors that should be considered when selecting a coach.

Your job is to pick someone that you think will help YOU achieve your goals. If it is important for you to see credentials behind a coach's name, then find someone that has those credentials. If not, you certainly can find a good coach without them. However, I'd make sure that they have enough experience to counterbalance their lack of certified training.

Personally, I like to see that coaches are actively pursuing ways to improve themselves and add value to their coaching practice with some form of training or certification.

Barbara Christensen owns Bija Coaching, a health and wellness practice. Here are the credentials she has by her name:

> Barbara Christensen , CPT, SN, HLWC, Aroma Coach

I didn't know what each of these credentials stood for until I looked them up. In my world a "CPT" is a Certified Performance Technologist. In Barbara's world that is a Certified Personal Coach. An HLWC is a Holistic Life and Wellness Coach. If you look up the requirements for each of the certifications you realize that the coach had to go through some effort to obtain these titles. These titles coupled with real experience should signal that you are getting someone who has taken the time to obtain formal training in their field. Combine this with the extensive research Barbara conducts each time she answers a health or wellness question and you've got your proof that you are working with a coach that deeply cares about ongoing learning toward helping her clients succeed. It also helps that she continues to produce books and blogposts that demonstrate her detailed knowledge and applied wisdom in her field.

Another example from some of the coaches in our online community is from Tanya Smith of Tanya Smith Online Coaching. She shares her education credentials, her certifications, and areas of expertise.

> Online Marketing
> Content Strategy
> Personal Branding
> Content Marketing
> Business Systems
> Social Media
>
> MBA, PHR, CCMC, CLTMC, CPBMC
> Florida State University
>
> content strategy   content marketing   business coach   small business   online branding   time management   business productivity   tanya smith   training   personal brand

I think this gives her a leg up in the world of online internet marketing. Though she focuses on coaching entrepreneurs, her MBA (master's in business administration), PHR (Professional in Human Resources Certification) and CLTMC (Certified Leadership and Talent Management Coach) are signals that she may also have experience implementing her coaching skills in larger organizations. Many corporations and organizations require their personnel to go through the process of obtaining these types of credentials. Or, corporate professionals seek these on their own to continue their own career growth. In a world where everyone claims marketing expertise, she offers skills and credentials to back up her claims. Plus, her website, online marketing and interactions demonstrate that she practices what she proclaims.

Do the credentials make coaches better coaches? Not necessarily. It is a continual balance between practice and learning the theory behind it. As an example, I have a project management professional (PMP) certification. I worked over ten years in project and program management roles before I even pursued the certification. While in a class preparing for the exam, I talked with some of the people that had just entered the field a few months before. And, they were taking the test alongside me. Their new credential will only take them so far. There must be experiences to back it up. In the case of project management, I know when I'm working with an experienced PM and when I'm working with someone with a freshly minted certificate. My experiences help me quickly differentiate between the two while also identifying someone that has mastered those areas of project management where I need to improve.

Over-credentialed Coaches

Does the coach have a list of credentials a mile long?

Buyers beware.

This is where I draw from years as a recruiter, hiring manager, and as a member of hiring teams. Too many courses and credentials start to signal someone that spends more time learning than practicing. Though it isn't bad practice to keep learning, some are addicted to endless training. At some point, the coach must get out and do the work. Through doing the work, the lessons are learned. The principles turn into application. They experience how to help different types of individuals improve their performance, they discern the different attributes they have that help or hurt their clients and can then focus on what areas they must continue to refine and improve to offer better coaching services.

I remember talking about this dilemma in graduate school when one of my professors had extremely strong feelings about all the adult learning theories we were researching in the course. I drew upon my years of substitute teaching experience across K-12 in all subject areas when I was taking the class. I pointed out to her that I found it fascinating to learn about all the theories, but once I walked into that classroom and the first student threw the spitball or called someone a name, I had to immediately think through a combination of solutions and practical methods to ensure there was a safe and effective environment for learning to take place. I drew upon theory to effectively manage and teach the class, but I also had to modify my on the ground approach every minute as different needs arose.

Such is the case with coaching. I love the idea that I heard expressed years ago that essentially boiled down to "one does not gain satisfaction out of endless training, one must perform." It can be invigorating to constantly learn new concepts, but those concepts cannot change or improve anything unless they are applied to a problem or situation. At that point we find out what happens when it is applied to real people with thoughts, feelings, skills, hang-ups, and imperfections.

As you consider this factor, make sure that if you are a credential lover, your coach has a balance between their professional certifications and relevant experience to demonstrate they can perform the work.

Learning Sources

Along these lines, find out who the coach learns from – their coaches and mentors, the books they read, the kinds of resources they draw upon to acquire their knowledge and advanced learning.

A coach I was working with started posting various comments and passages on Facebook from people that I don't respect. At first it didn't bother me, but then it became a trend. Were these the people the coach drew upon for guidance and inspiration? Is this who they turned to for additional expertise?

This could fall into the factor related to values, but it is important to ask these questions as you determine how important their sources of information are toward helping you progress.

Certification and Training Questions to Ponder

- What kinds of training and certifications do they pursue? Other learning opportunities?
- Are these sources considered credible by those in their field?
- Do they have a combination of credentials and experience?
- Are their experiences and certifications in balance?
- What types of learning and inspirational sources do they follow?

THE REFERRAL

In the business of referrals, trust is the most important reason a recommendation is made and, conversely, lack of trust the single greatest reason referrals don't happen.
~ John Jantsch, The Referral Engine and Duct Tape Marketing

"You must work with them! They are an awesome coach!"

Many of us belong to a variety of groups and communities – work, home, clubs, church, special interests, etc. Each have a different focus. If you meet with a few people regularly for church, they know you in one context. But, perhaps they wouldn't recognize you if they saw you participating in a local bowling league or at a technology conference. Of course, if you are both there this could signal a mutual interest, right?

Remember when you were in grade school and saw one of your schoolteachers at the grocery store? Most of us were shocked to see that some of them were completely unrecognizable outside of the school setting. Some wore short shorts (men and women), others had questionable friends and still others seemed to be way richer than we supposed a schoolteacher could be (wealthy spouse, side gig or good spending habits?). The point being that some of the people that we consider close in our lives, may just know us from one dimension and might not have a clue as to what we already know and do. Some of my friends think that I'd love to go with them on a walk in the woods because I like the outdoors. No, not really. I like to be out walking in the sunshine and am completely fine if the closest tree is within a 500-foot radius of me in case I need a minute of shade. You have these nuances that even your closest friends won't pick up on unless they happen to be with you on the actual hike. It is then entirely possible that those closest to you may not realize that people they refer to you may not be a perfect fit. In fact, you might be able to coach the coach they are suggesting you follow!

A friend of a friend that refers you to a coach may not provide you any extra motivation to select the coach. On the other hand, you might accept that information if you look at the person's website or materials and they appear to validate the claims of the referral.

So, along with all the other factors to consider, remember that all referrals are not created equal. The closer someone is to knowing your preferences, your weaknesses, your strengths, and your goals, the better chance you have of them introducing you to someone that would meet those needs. That, of course, assumes that they are well connected and have your best intentions at heart. Nowadays affiliate marketing and friends owing someone a favor could play into this as well. Use your best judgment.

Note: Affiliates

The marketing masses are catching on that it is smart to partner with other entrepreneurs to promote each other. This has always been part of the social and business economy. However, the new technology tools make it even easier to set up these relationships. You may find yourself constantly assessing whether you are being introduced to someone that is the best fit for you or if they are just in an affiliate relationship with that coach. Affiliate relationships are lucrative for the coaches and for those that introduce new clients to them. This isn't bad, but it could be bad for you. You may be connected to a perfectly good coach for someone else, but they may not be right for you.

Pay attention to those referring you to coaches. Do they try to partner with everyone, or do they appear selective in who they choose to highlight?

In 2001, I was looking for a graduate program to further my schooling. I'd been out in the workforce for a while and thought it would help me if I went back and got an MBA. So, I applied, got accepted, and started taking courses at University of Maryland. My first course was accounting and didn't get me too thrilled about the program. Still, I was determined to make a go of it and so I finished that course and enrolled for the next set of courses in my cohort.

It was during this time that Tonya Barnett, a former co-worker and friend, emailed me out of the blue. She forwarded an email about an immersive graduate experience offered by George Mason University in Northern Virginia. It was focused on instructional systems design and technologies.

It looked interesting because it combined my love of teaching, training, online technologies, and innovation all in one program. I applied and was accepted before I even realized what I was getting into.

I dropped out of the University of Maryland and started my classes at George Mason University within a few months of my friend's email. When I walked into my first two classes, I had no idea what really was involved in the program. Adult learning theory, HTML, graphic design, an engineering process for creating learning products, project management? What was all this stuff? Was I in the right place?

Perhaps I am the first person in the world that skimmed an email from a friend and signed up for a graduate program. It says a lot about that friend, doesn't it? This person had been a trainer with me in college. She knew my background and interests. She thought highly of my training experience. She had been enrolled in the program and knew that it could be the right fit for me.

I believed her and acted. Sure, there was probably a bit of a heavenly nudge involved. It ended up being exactly what I needed.

In selecting a coach, you do need the help of friends, co-workers or even other coaches. If you don't have friends that know of great coaches, then it is time to start small. Join a few Facebook and LinkedIn groups. Watch how the different coaches interact with others in the group. Visit their websites. Connect with them on Twitter. Ask them a question and analyze their response. Find out what people are saying about them. Find out if anyone you know is connected to them and find out more.

Over time you will be able to see how they respond to potential clients and clients and discern if they are the best fit for you.

Referrals are the most lucrative form of business for successful coaches. Many of them can substantially reduce their marketing budget if they continue to provide great coaching services to their individual clients. Good news travels quick and far. Though there are some pitfalls to consider in this area, I recommend placing referral recommendations as one of those factors to keep at the top of your list when sifting through a list of potential coaches.

Referral Questions to Ponder

- Do you trust the judgement of the person referring you to the coach?
- What kinds of gut reaction/feelings did you have when you first interacted with the coach directly/indirectly (e.g. website, blogposts, responses to those asking them questions)?
- Do you notice others referring the coach you are considering?
- Is it clear who they are affiliated with? And, are those connections clearly relevant to their offerings?
- Are they connected to other experienced mentors and coaches?

PERSONALITY

Personality has power to uplift, power to depress, power to curse, and power to bless.

~ Paul Harris

Interviewing candidates for corporate positions is always an enlightening experience for me. Those applicants that make it to the interview stage have resumes that have made it through multiple vetting processes, at least in my organization. They've remained because their experiences, the organizations they worked for, their educational pursuits, and sometimes a hobby have seemed impressive on paper. And, then they enter the room for the interview. Wow! Sometimes the interview panel must do a double take after the interview begins to make sure that the right resume is being used for the discussion. Clearly, resume writing services are effective at getting people in the door. But, once in the door you must back that up with a comparable real you!

I had an interesting experience recruiting a financial expert. After three full days of interviewing candidates face-to-face, I was anxious (and so was the rest of the hiring panel) to wrap up the discussions and select a final candidate. We'd had a few people that we thought would work well. After a brief break, we prepared for the last interview of the day. Her resume had the usual impressive experiences and yet we knew that our conversation would bring out the strengths and weaknesses quickly.

The woman walked in the room with a strong presence – well suited, attractive hair style, basically friendly and well kept. But, when she opened her mouth we sat in awe as she simultaneously made us feel like old friends while also expressing clearly the leadership strategies and financial insights she practiced on a day-to-day basis. She regularly interacted with Senators and Congressmen as well as the financial analysts in the cube farms. Her responses and questions demonstrated complete confidence from experience and an openness to learning.

When this woman left the room, the members of our panel turned to each other and each of us made the same comment – "Wow. I want her to mentor me!"

There are some people that just light up a room. Their warmth, their charisma, and their interest in people are invigorating and contagious. It is even better when you feel that warmth directed at you and you feel like the most handsome, most beautiful, smartest, clever or innovative person in their presence. Or, at least you have a moment where you feel like you have the capability to become that person.

Like it or not, personality can disrupt all the criteria on the list. It is difficult to look beyond it even if we think we are committed to learning a skill that only a die-hard, egotistical, self-centered, bully can teach us.

So, this is a tough one because the mind easily glides over big glaring weaknesses when someone has a personality that we fall in love with and want to work around. Have you heard about doctors with a great "bedside manner?" Often patients rate them as smarter and better doctors even if this isn't the case based upon their history.

How important this is requires going back to what you are looking for – a coach to push you hard with a bit of tough love? A coach that can support you in a personal area where you feel "broken?" A cheerleader?

> A coach is someone who can give correction
> without causing resentment.
> ~ *John Wooden, Basketball Coach*

This is tricky, but at the same time it can be the easiest part of selecting a coach. You are either drawn to a personality or you are not. Occasionally, you may have enough exposure to someone that they kind of grow on you, but usually this is a visceral decision.

This is where our brains can fail us again. You could be focusing too much on personality. Remember, you are picking a coach. Not a best friend. Not a spouse. And, at the same time not a boss or a parent. This is someone that is supposed to ensure that you get to your end goal. First impressions are important, but take a step back for a minute.

Some of the most motivating teachers and coaches in my life have been those that have had extremely high expectations of me. I felt it. I knew they thought I could do it and I found that I could. Others were extremely tough, but weren't motivating to me. They had a chip on their shoulder, were self-centered or were more worried about appearing to be the tough coach than translating that toughness into helping me improve. Still others were tough and a bit rough around the edges, but I knew they cared deep down. Their personality just hid their interest, and capabilities, in helping me make massive changes.

The type of coaching you need also matters. If you need coaching to help change your life after a rough patch or some serious depression, a soothing and rah-rah cheerleader type coach might be exactly the type of coaching you need at that time. If you are trying to up your game in business, sports, or influence, you may want someone that pushes you with constructive criticism, tough love, and intense goal deadlines.

Personality Questions to Ponder

- What teacher or coach motivated you to perform better? Why?
- Do you do well with someone that is a hard driver, or gives you a periodic pep talk, or focused on giving a gentle push in the right direction?
- Are you open to being pushed when you are feeling de-motivated or do you hold that against the person?
- Are you negatively affected by someone who is too blunt? Or, does it give you that extra push to prove to them (and yourself) that you can and will do it?

HOLD ME ACCOUNTABLE

Accountability breeds response-ability.

~ Stephen Covey

Coaches have different approaches for holding you accountable. One of my group coaches was very flexible and supportive, but perhaps a little too easy. She didn't address my late monthly "homework" assignments the first few months of the year and I started to slack off. How does a motivated person like me slack off when I'm paying $250 a month for coaching support? I didn't feel like I was held accountable, and I had access to all the coaching materials indefinitely. I dutifully downloaded the materials and videos to my computer each month as they were available. I figured that at least I got the content I'd paid for even if I was late on homework and was missing some of the group coaching calls. Sure, my life was beyond busy, but I was paying $250 on a tight budget for this coaching. I needed to get something out of it.

What would have happened if she was a little bit tougher in that first month or two? If she had reached out through email to ask if she could assist me or to find out if I was stuck? I think that I would have felt more compelled to participate and make it a priority for myself. On her end, she could have demonstrated that she was aware of my personal goals and reached out to ask a few more questions. After all, I paid her for one year of services.

Most of the responsibility falls on me, but from a coaching perspective, the coach should want the client to achieve as much success as possible in their coaching program. And, not just for personal reasons, but for good business. Clients that are held accountable and succeed start to spread the word. They become great referral partners and provide excellent free marketing! As it was, I did get a lot out of the coaching, but it was all at the end of the year when I had a break at Thanksgiving and Christmas. I was finally able to sit down and listen to all the recordings and read through the homework assignments. If I had been better engaged each month, I would have made greater strides in personal progress. I would have completed multiple products, contributed more to the group coaching sessions and built a stronger network of relationships with her other clients. It was my loss, but it was also hers. No matter how great her new programs appear, I now know that her approach to accountability isn't a fit for me.

Though we've talked about this in the personality section, it bears repeating again. The personality of the coach matters. So, does their accountability style. If they can take the time (and it does take time and commitment) to hold you accountable, they really can help you achieve more in your goals than you'd ever believe.

John Wooden, a long-time basketball coach for UCLA, became famous for his success in turning mediocre teams into high performing championship winners. He didn't walk into a talent goldmine when he started coaching most teams. In fact, usually it was just the opposite. These weren't the top recruits and they certainly didn't have great facilities or sponsors supporting them. In fact, when he started coaching at UCLA, he had better coaching opportunities come along, but turned them down because he had already committed to UCLA.

Wooden took the time to care about each player enough to hold them accountable for the small things, even down to how they wore their socks and tied their shoes. What? How they wore their socks and tied their shoes? How would that help? Well, if you've ever played basketball (or other sports for that matter), do you know how annoying it is if your sock is too loose, too tight, too low? Do you remember what kinds of chaffing or blistering can occur if they are out of place? What happens if the shoes become untied (or you feel like they might be) right when you are to perform your best? You aren't focused on the goal, are you? No, you are worried about what is happening with a minor physical disturbance going on in your shoe! Wrong focus.

I love that story because it shows that sometimes we don't like when people are picky about the small things or ask us about the small details of what we are doing. And, I've had experience playing basketball and know how annoying an untied shoelace or tight sock can feel at the wrong moment.
Following up on the small things matters. It is often where the greatest

change takes place. If someone is willing to follow up with us on the small stuff, we can get focused and clearer on doing the small stuff correctly. We start to care about every action we take. Hopefully not in a way that creates fear, but in a way that encourages us to take risks, learn from our mistakes and keep perfecting whatever it is that we are pursuing. When we look back, we see that small steps have led to big results.

Careless About Accountability

One of the weaknesses of online coaches is that many get careless with accountability. Unfortunately, as they grow and take on more clients, their ability to be effective at holding you and other clients accountable seems to diminish. Some have figured out a way to hire teams of people to follow up with you when they cannot take time for the individual session with you. However, some of these team members are inconsistent. Typical of my experience at the ranch, some of them are paid minimum wage to maintain customer relationships and continue to up sell you to different coaching packages. Your ability to get the benefits of a live coach becomes harder and harder and therefore … far more expensive for you when you do desire to get more of their time.

Make sure to ask if you will be held accountable by the coach or by a team member they've hired.

Sometimes it is worth going with someone that has a lot of experience but are more obscure and picky about how they spend their time. Once they commit, they will be available to hold you accountable.

In the world of online coaches, pay attention to how the products and services change as a coach takes on a larger web presence and more clients. Take special note of how you feel you are being treated.

It is important to note here that there is nothing wrong with coaches hiring out a team of coaches to represent their brand and deliver their services. Typically, these supporting coaches do go through personal training with the primary coach in what style and approach that they should use to represent the brand. Some may end up better at coaching than the original coach. It is important to be informed in this area. If these teams of coaches have less experience than their senior coaches, the coaching pricing should reflect that difference and it should be clearly marketed so that you are aware of the distinction before you purchase.

Staying attentive and providing accountability to "the one" is a very difficult area for many of the coaches that started their careers during this era of online coaching. Some are so anxious to build their online presence and accumulate clients that they can lose focus on the individual client in search of a systematic process of coaching and funneling clients through a uniform approach. Don't get me wrong. I am a process lover! However, when you pursue a goal, it will be messy. And, you and the coach must be able to work together to navigate those areas of the plan that don't end up following "the process" well, but that do bring big spurts of growth.

So, a few key tips about looking for accountability:

- Ensure the coach has a clear plan to hold you accountable (e.g. approach to follow-up, what tools they will use, frequency of follow-up)
- Helps you set realistic goals and/or modify the goals you've already chosen.
- Provide relevant helps along the way (e.g. support, links to resources, connections to people) that demonstrate that they are actively engaged in your goal achieving process
- Bold Follow-up – they don't have to be THAT tough, but they do need to be bold in their follow-up. Why didn't you work on the goal this week? What are you going to do differently? What got in the way of you accomplishing your goal? Let's plan for next week.
- Questions and discussions with you at each point in the process to ensure you are making progress and not just going through their pre-defined coaching process.

Accountability is an essential part of growth. No matter how committed and smart you are, it is amazing how often you can justify yourself out of making progress on a goal that you set for yourself. Coaches provide that external support to ensure that you make that progress you know you need to make to become your best self. As a side note, accountability partners are important too. They aren't paid like your coach, but are another mechanism that can support you on your road to success. More about that in another book that I wrote.

Accountability Questions to Ponder

- Are you feeling more accountable?
- Is your coach personally helping you set more realistic goals?
- Are they following up with you every time?
- Are they available to send you resources they run across that may be of interest to you and your goal?
- Are they available if you say you have a special need to discuss your lack of progress?

ADMINISTRATIVE

> Thank your customer for complaining and mean it.
> Most will never bother to complain. They'll just walk away.
>
> ~ *Marilyn Suttle*

Before the Internet era, we relied on a simple calendar and phone to schedule appointments and ensure a product was delivered on time. Now, most coaches leverage technology to schedule their coaching sessions, sell online products and collect payment for all their products and services. Online tools are great, but unless the humans behind them constantly monitor and adjust them, they can have an impact on the success of the coach and the customer experience. The resources, after all, should never be the product when it comes to coaching. It should be a supporting option to the service the coach is offering. If the tool is the product, then just go buy access to an online website or download an app for $4.99. This isn't active coaching. Detailed insight and support on how to use a product, however, may count as training or coaching.

A few years ago, I signed up to receive "old" content from a coach each month. It was $4.95 and seemed like no big deal. The first month I received the link to the content and downloaded as much of it as I could. It was great! All of that for $4.95 – what a deal! A few months passed by and

I tried to log in to see if there was some new "old" content. The link didn't work. I contacted the support email address I was provided and didn't get an answer for a couple of weeks. By then I had forgotten about it because it was one of those minor charges each month that I barely noticed.

A year went by. I started going through all my accounts and cleaning up those pesky little monthly charges. I couldn't even find the link to the old content and requested that I be removed from the service since I wasn't getting any content anyway. The administrative staff that responded said that they couldn't do anything on their end. I'd have to go through PayPal to stop the charge. I thought this was a little strange since you should be able to have them stop charging you for a product or service you aren't receiving. So, I contacted PayPal who then had me contact the real credit card it was coming through and after numerous attempts, multiple complaints and a few hairs pulled out of my head, the charges stopped. Remember, this was only $4.95 a month. So, anything more than five minutes spent on this felt extremely wasteful of my time. If I counted my hourly rate as a charge for the time spent, it would have been about $500.00 - $1,000.00 worth of effort. Almost better to leave the charge on until I cut up the credit card and cancelled the account…which I admit, I thought about doing. The coach is an amazing coach. I had listened to her CDs and watched her online video programs and really did enjoy her. She had a message that she was brilliant at sharing. But, the administrative corrections I went through were unnecessarily painful. What a shame that someone who has such greatness to offer is losing business because they can't get a few basic back office things in order. I will continue to use her free and one-time purchase products, but I'm still leery of what I may experience if we work together in the future. Unfortunately, it tainted my coaching experience with her.

Regardless of how amazing someone is, find out how the entire experience works. It's just like personal relationships. If a friend consistently needs to borrow money from you or doesn't seem to have enough to pay the bill when you go out to eat, you tire of going anywhere with them that requires spending money. They could be talented, friendly and interesting. But, after a while that doesn't seem to matter. You just move on.

Through my work in product development in a large organization, I've learned how much the sustainment of a product can really cost. Generally, the upfront cost is always the smallest part of the investment. The ongoing maintenance of a product are lifecycle costs that really add up over time. Experienced coaches that use systems and tools understand this, sometimes through hard experience over time. It's never once and done. It's once and then again and again and again. Products must be discarded, edited, re-created, etc. All of that takes time, energy, and money. And, if the coach doesn't have a good overall system of administration all that work falls on them which can become a distraction in their capability to give full attention to what they are good at – coaching!

Administrative Questions to Ponder

- How does the coach respond to complaints or questions?

- Do they make any promises to you as a customer – response time promises, service level agreements, refunds?
- Do they have a system/approach set up that streamlines the customer experience for you?
- Is the online process clear to you? Do you have to think about it or is it intuitive?
- Do they appear, or state, that they are working with others to manage their online presence or do they mentioning taking this all on themselves?

RELIABLE

Employ every economy consistent with thoroughness, accuracy and reliability.
~ Arthur C. Nielsen

Just like the administrative details that can quickly erode trust, some free-spirited coaches may have an issue with dependability. They may have flexible schedules on their end, but they shouldn't treat you like yours has the same flexibility.

I've had coaches completely forget about our call, arrive 15 minutes late for 30-minute sessions (and made sure they end on time), and those that I've signed up with and never heard from again. One coach didn't even login to present her materials for a virtual conference I created. A complete no show.

It sounds kind of crazy, especially for someone that is in the business of helping people reach their goals. Coaches aren't being paid for filling a space, like toll booth operators on turnpikes or mall shop employees on Tuesday evenings. Those are employees – stuck in place in case someone arrives for business. Coaches are all about showing up at the right time and place to share the right information and support.

Certainly, there will be an excuse here and there, but if you hear (or see) this as a pattern, it might be time to find someone who is anxious to serve you and help you progress in your goals at the agreed upon time and place.

Reliable Questions to Ponder

- Has anyone mentioned a lack of dependability with this coach?
- Do you know anyone connected to them that can provide insights into their reliability with coaching calls and follow-up?
- Are they consistent in their messages and responsiveness to customers? Responsive to you before you are a client?
- Do they show up on time? Do you?

COMMUNICATION

The more elaborate our means of communication,

the less we communicate.

~ Joseph Priestley

Video is a powerful way to connect with others and so many coaches like to use it in their individual and group coaching sessions. One coach had a live video chat taking place on Facebook and suddenly got excited that one of her students was listening in and asked to put her on the screen. The participant fumbled about a bit and finally appeared on the screen. She obviously hadn't planned on being seen during the call and everyone could tell she was uncomfortable. Even if the participant felt that video was a great method, she would have appreciated a heads up in this situation so she could bring her best self to the interaction. Instead of being able to focus on the coaching, her focus was diverted to worrying about how she looked, and it was clear she was quietly adjusting her screen so that we wouldn't see parts of her messy house in the background.

I love email and texting. I manage dozens of teams primarily through emails and conference calls, but only get in one-on-one phone conversations when necessary. Do you think I'd pick a coach that only communicated with me through the phone? No way. Our collaborations would most likely fail.

It's important to find a coach that communicates in ways that are best for YOU.

It is great to "hope" that an approach will work for you, but even better to select your coach based upon how they already communicate and appeal to your communication preferences. As you get experience working with coaches, it might be good to branch out into other communication methods. But, if you are just getting started, select someone that will be the easiest for you to follow up with and will enhance your chances for success. There is no need to add extra anxiety to the coaching experience. You've taken a big step to get help. Make that step easier by selecting someone that communicates in a way that is comfortable for you and with the same communication tools.

At times a coach is willing to communicate with you using your preferred communication methods, and not theirs. Buyers beware. You are putting your coach out of their most effective and comfortable zone. That will have an impact on your coaching relationship. It also means that the coach will spend some additional time, and possible worry, on how they coach you. That time is better spent specifically on the growth you want to obtain by working with the coach than trying to adjust the coach to meet your needs. There are thousands of coaches out there and you can easily go apply your list of criteria to finding a coach that best fits you!

...an exception to this rule

There is one exception to this rule. If you have a goal to improve and/or use a certain communication method more, then you should agree on that method as a matter of principle and practice. It may be slightly uncomfortable, but if it is part of your goal.... a little discomfort can soon be overcome with practice! Make sure to let the coach know this is an area you are working to improve if it isn't clearly stated in your coaching arrangement.

Communication Options

Typical communication tools used by coaches include all the old favorites (e.g. the phone) and a few new (e.g. Facebook Live). These can be used in both live interactions (e.g. video streaming) and accessed as needed (e.g. pre-recorded audio/video, text message, email).

Common ways to communicate include:
- Face-to-face
- Phone – personal or group conference call – using services like freeconferencecall.com
- Email
- Text Message
- Webinars – through online services such as ClickMeeting, GotoMeeting, Webex, AdobeConnect,
- Live video streaming – Skype, Google Hangout, Zoom
- Websites and Membership Sites – logins to specific pages where

commenting and collaborating take place. Online communities – closed or open groups that allow for clients to interact with each other and the coach. Popular examples include Facebook Groups, LinkedIn Groups, etc.

Communication is essential in day-to-day life and even more so in a coaching relationship. Like values, it is important that you and your coach are compatible. This is an area where both of you need to be able to operate in your optimal zone. Don't try to cut corners on this one.

Communications Questions to Ponder

- What communication methods do you prefer? Email, texting, phone, live video? A combination of communication methods? Real-time or delayed (asynchronous)?
- Does the coach you are considering have a style that will fit your typical approach to communicating?
- Do they define their preferences and communication approach? They should and most do. Please pay careful attention to how they communicate and how this is incorporated into the products and services they offer.

NETWORK AND RESOURCES

Since you cannot do good to all, you are to pay special attention to those who, by the accidents of time, or place, or circumstances, are brought into closer connection with you.

~ Saint Augustine

It's common for a coach to offer additional value beyond individual or group coaching. There are mailing lists, online communities (like Facebook groups, LinkedIn groups, etc.) and mastermind small groups that they often offer in combination with their services.

It is up to you to take advantage of these opportunities, and I suggest that you do.

Why?

Coaches are connected to other people like you. People seeking improvement and change. People paying for services. People that may be future connections for you!

Many coaches offer similar services, but some of the ways they can set themselves apart is their approach and their personal network. If you can become part of their network, you will not only learn from those groups and connections, but you may also find a joint venture partner, a new affiliate relationship, the right person to help you with something your business needs or a chance to be the right person for someone in that network.

I often tell people that selecting a coach that gives you access to their network is one of the most valuable services that a coach has to offer. The individual attention is obviously important, but to gain access to their network can lead to amazing opportunities down the line. Of course, there will be a price to finding a coach with a great network that fits your needs.

I've been given access to a few private coaching groups over the past few years. Some of them had experienced authors, entrepreneurs, tech moguls and non-profit leaders. Others were filled with people that were all at the beginner level in their field. It might provide comfort to be surrounded with people with equal or less expertise, but the more you pay for the coach, the higher expectation you should have of the exclusive network. If you do your homework, and you see evidence of being introduced to a high quality and experienced group of people, pay the higher price for the coach to get access to their personal network.

Resources

As part of being of a network, you also gain exposure to great resources that they know about or provide. Coaches should be sharing a variety of resources with you. If they are doing their homework, they'll know the latest books, podcasts, seminars, and websites that will help provide you additional support on your journey.

In the right networks, you can even connect directly to the authors and producers of some of the resources that are shared.

Network and Resources Questions to Ponder

- Do you know anyone in the coach's network? Can they share with you the experience/success level of the network?
- Does the coach specifically identify access to a group or network as part of their service?
- Does the coach regularly share connections with their potential clients or existing online communities that are open to you?
- Does the coach only share affiliate information or regularly connect their communities to people/resources with no strings attached (no affiliate relationship)?
- Will the coach interact in other communities online or only push their network or community?

PRODUCT PORTFOLIO

*In the end, all business operations can be
reduced to three words: people, product, and profits.*

~ Lee Iacocca

The portfolio is one of those factors that may be invaluable in selecting a coach. If you were to just select a coach from a word of mouth referral without referencing their website, looking them up on LinkedIn or "Googling" their name, you wouldn't have any concept of how the experience works until you were already in the coaching relationship. Thank goodness it is part of most online strategies to give you access to them multiple ways before you enter a coaching relationship with them.

Most coaches have a website. On the website they typically offer a free download to an eBook or checklist that they think you will find valuable. This gives you a chance to review their work and approach. They may have a YouTube or Vimeo channel where they share tips, tricks and insights related to their area of expertise. They may have a book or a small video series that you can purchase for as cheaply as $2.99 (many Amazon Kindle eBooks) or for somewhere in the range of $29-$49. They may even hold free webinars for potential clients or a free coaching session to find out if you are both the right fit for each other.

Take advantage of these opportunities! Not because you are cheap. You need to access these materials to give you a feel for their experience, personality, approach, personal style, etc. In other words, it gives you a way to assess them based upon the factors you are learning about in this book!

Find out what happens after you select them as a coach. Do they continue to provide their clients freebies? Do they provide discounted offers to their other services and products? You can find this out from those that have already been coached by them, but many have these discounts openly posted on their websites. If it isn't clear from either of these methods, ask them what special products and services are available to those that have become a client.

Of course, all products and services aren't created equal. Some coaches crank out a lot of free stuff that isn't that valuable. Or, claim that you will have access to a network of people in online groups that have very little actual networking or knowledge sharing taking place. But, I'm saying that as I remember my retreat experience. What one-person thinks should be free, another may find invaluable. Luckily, it is up to you to decide!

It's great to have so much access to information about coaches right now. But, it's tough to discern based upon the online presence. Some coaches have outdone themselves and their product portfolio is beautiful with little substance. Some have great materials that don't look great. You will experience trial and error in this area and even with experience you'll still have some hit and miss experiences. Learn from it. Take what you can learn from whatever you purchase and over time the value you receive should be greater than any of the $29 failed purchases you make.

Product Portfolio Questions to Ponder

- Is their website professional and demonstrate they have thought through all the layers of support expected of coaches in today's environment (e.g. freebies, clear communication, examples and samples, blogposts/podcasts to see their content, clear product explanations/illustrations, etc.)
- Is there too much marketing and not enough substance on the website and product descriptions?
- Are they clear on what differentiates them from others (e.g. what is their value proposition if they are a social media marketing coach)?
- Are there other feedback mechanisms, other than their own website, for testimonials (e.g. Amazon reviews of books, posts from trusted sources on reputable sites, social media comments, etc.)?

TIME

> The future is something which everyone reaches at the rate
> of 60 minutes an hour, whatever he does, whoever he is.
> ~ C. S. Lewis

Time is valuable. Most of us don't feel like we have enough of it. However, if you want to get coaching, it is going to take time. Selecting the right coach has a lot to do with the amount of time you are willing to invest in the endeavor. This oft times has nothing to do with your personal feelings about committing. It simply has to do with how many other obligations you have signed up for in your life. Family, friends, work, church, community activities, online activities, exercise and vacations are just a few of the priorities that make up our lives. Add to that our personality type and our energy levels and this all can add up to very little spare time for our coaching support needs.

There is a point, however, where you must cut or delay another priority if you are truly serious about getting the coaching you need to improve your performance in a certain area.

Luckily, you have options! There are many types of coaches out there and you should be able to find one that fits your specific needs.

Commitment Level

Perhaps you should find a coach that checks in by text once a week after you've read an online lesson. Or, maybe you'd be better with a coach that offers individual and group sessions. Or, maybe you need more one-on-one guidance in real-time.

There are so many combinations out there to choose from right now. *The bottom line is this – the more one-on-one coaching you seek, the higher the price.* You often have access to more accountability and a higher return on your personal investment.

Here is a general breakdown of what online coaches typically offer. This is very general, but it is surprising how many of them follow a similar approach. They must all be learning from the same marketing coaches.

Minimal Commitment

- Monthly coaching call – follow-up on progress, assign next steps
- Weekly message from the coach (e.g. automatic email, automatic video message, text message)
- Access to the coach's private online community (e.g. Facebook group)
- Free access to ongoing webinars.

Typical Commitment

- 1-2 Monthly coaching calls – follow-up on progress, assign next steps. One of these sessions may be a group coaching session.
- Weekly message from the coach (e.g. automatic email, automatic video message, text message)
- Access to the coach's private online community network (e.g. Facebook group)
- Access to a private membership site (often an additional re-occurring monthly expense OR a larger one-time expense if it houses a course)
- Discounts or periodic inclusions to special retreats or virtual conferences.
- Free access to ongoing webinars. This may also be part of the group coaching sessions that often occur by webinar.

Getting Serious Commitment

- 2-4 Monthly coaching calls – follow-up on progress, assign next steps.
- Group coaching sessions – this is where you can get some real value from the coach's network.
- Mastermind groups – this could tie in with the group coaching sessions provided, but often these are more often a variety of other coaches and outside people that are seeking accountability and networking opportunities.
- Weekly message from the coach (e.g. automatic email, automatic video message, text message)

- Access to the coach's private online community network (e.g. Facebook group)
- Access to a private membership site (often an additional re-occurring monthly expense OR a unique course and/or past content)
- Discounts or periodic inclusions to special retreats or virtual conferences.
- Free access to ongoing webinars. This may also be part of the group coaching sessions that often occur by webinar.
- Perk – if the coach discovers you have talents in certain areas that they'd like to leverage, many coaches have recruited some of their best/favorite/unique clients to work for them, with them, or in conjunction with other opportunities.

You can start to see that a lot of coaching nowadays isn't just a weekly phone call or a communication through one channel. Coaches use a combination of methods and all take …time. Using these methods aren't always right for you or others, but many are following it because it is the most lucrative and time saving approach for the coach.

Some of us are busy. Ok, who are we kidding? We are all busy. Sometimes we don't want to watch webinars, join conference calls, send back and forth emails and have access to private membership sites. Sometimes we just want to be coached! On the other hand, some of you may be craving more interactions and connections and may thrive in arrangements where you have numerous ways to connect with the coach. And, as shared before – access to their network.

It is worth mentioning again. Don't feel like you must select an approach that will overwhelm you or will rob you of the exact coaching you need. Keep shopping if the approach the coach uses isn't the right fit. There are hundreds of other coaches that may offer products and services just the way you need them.

Time of Day

What also plays into this area is time of day. Some of us work full-time and must have our conference calls or communications in the evening or weekends. Others are working at home and have more flexibility.

One of my coaches has regular sessions in the middle of the day on Mondays. I'm not quite her target audience, but I do like her work. So, I'm often not able to attend the group sessions on Mondays. However, I can watch the recordings. I have determined that it works for me, but that is because I'm signed up with her for a short-term need and it isn't a primary area of focus for me. If the goals I was working on were my focus, this wouldn't be the coach for me. I wouldn't even be available to be fully present and participate during the key timeframes that the expected interactions need to take place.

Time in Life

We typically grasp time of day, but it is sometimes a bit harder to grasp if something is right for our life timing. There are realities for different points in our lives that must be taken into consideration when we think about time.

Is it a good idea to train for a marathon when we are three months pregnant? We might have the right amount of time available and the trainer might be available for us at the right time of day, but seriously there are some important factors to consider when making a choice like this. As I'm writing this, I am pregnant. I've only had miscarriages up to this point in my life and I'm over 40 years old. There is NO WAY that I'm going to take the risk of training for a marathon right now. I feel like I have this one chance to do it right and it isn't worth the risk. Once the tiny person is born, it's a different story. It might be the absolute perfect time to train for the marathon because I'll be focused on losing weight, getting healthy and even spending more time outdoors.

Sometimes we are impatient with ourselves and want to complete all our goals now.

A few years ago, I took care of some of my nieces and nephews while my sister and her husband took a much-needed vacation. Yes, I signed up to babysit six children for 10 days! I've been working full-time outside of the home for over 20 years. I'm accustomed to doing a lot of MY stuff during the day. But, I learned very quickly that it caused extra anxiety for me if I tried to do my projects and take care of the nieces and nephews during the same hours of the day. It made me angry and got them all riled up. And, rightfully so. I wasn't being attentive to them. After a day or two I figured out that they were very good at marching off to bed to read books and go to sleep between 8:00 – 8:30 p.m. each evening. So, I made that my personal project time. It made a world of difference! I focused on them and the home management during the day. I worked on my projects at night. Win-Win!

Now, obviously I was just babysitting for two weeks. However, it taught me a great lesson about the times and seasons of our lives. It may be acceptable to put off a goal or two for a season if there are other priorities that must take precedence. But, keep those goals close so that you don't regret not pursuing them. If they are important, it may be worth making other sacrifices like getting help (e.g. babysitter, someone to clean the house each week/month, etc.) to free you up to pursue that goal that is important to your personal growth.

Time Questions to Ponder

- Does the coach offer just the right amount of coaching support for your needs?
- Do their offerings match your availability (e.g. days, times, frequency)?
- Are you shifting your life commitments around more than you normally do to meet the coaching schedule? Is that a sustainable approach for you currently?
- If this coach is particularly important to you, what ways can you make changes in your life schedule for a period so that you can maximize the experience for your best benefit?
- How long are you willing to make changes in your personal schedule to work with a coach if they are optimal in every other way for you?

CONFIDENTIALITY - THE HUMAN VAULT

The human heart has hidden treasures, In secret kept, in silence sealed; The thoughts, the hopes, the dreams, the pleasures, Whose charms were broken if revealed.

~ Charlotte Bronte

A vault is a place you protect something that is valuable to you. For me it may be personal journals and to you it may be a pile of precious coins. Either way, there is typically a mechanism (e.g. lock) to allow the right people to access it and to keep the wrong people from accessing, damaging, or stealing it from the person securing the item.

Some people are great vaults. I was amazed at how much a couple of my roommates were able to keep secret when someone asked them not to divulge personal information. I gained great respect for them and have since become a better vault myself. Unfortunately, there are ways we can also become a vault in unintended ways. Many become vault like because they have felt like someone has made a significant breach in sharing their personal information at some point in life. They know how it feels to be exposed and become better at protecting private information. I will admit to having a few cracks in this area in the past, but am constantly working toward improving. There are things that I know that I will never share, even in those moments where I know it would satisfy a social urge to do so.

Coaches are interacting with you in very personal ways. They are helping you discern your deepest desires, talents, and passions. You expose to them thoughts and dreams that you may not feel comfortable sharing with the general public.

So, it is important to see how they act in the public forum and to observe if they refrain from sharing confidential information about others or themselves.

Keeping information confidential is an area that has taken on heightened monitoring and compliance as cybercrimes, online bullying, and general access to electronic files become a part of day-to-day existence. It is more important to factor in the human vault attribute in your decision-making.

Confidentiality Questions to Ponder

- Do they divulge too much about their clients?
- Do they act (online and offline environments) in ways that you consider inappropriate?
- How do they respond/react in controversial topics in private or public settings? Or, when they disagree?

EMOTIONAL INTELLIGENCE

> Emotional intelligence is a different way of being smart.
> It includes knowing what your feelings are and using your feelings to make good decisions in life. It's being able to manage distressing moods well and control impulses. It's being motivated and remaining hopeful and optimistic when you have setbacks in working toward goals. It's empathy; knowing what the people around you are feeling. And its social skill—getting along well with other people, managing emotions in relationships, being able to persuade or lead others.
>
> ~ *O'Neil*

This leads well into a discussion about emotional intelligence.

One day at the office, I was waiting for a meeting to begin and a computer programmer and a game designer were sitting and waiting with me. I work with dozens of teams on a regular basis and they all consist of a few technology types, a few management types and a few designer types. Different brains, different experiences and different education levels. The topic of emotional intelligence came up. For some reason I reacted strongly when I found out that none of them knew what that meant. My response did not demonstrate that I had high emotional intelligence and I ended up sending them an apology for acting like they didn't know anything. To be fair, their communication approach was often abrupt and lacking in emotional intelligence and so I was matching my style to theirs. Not very good timing on my part.

Emotional intelligence has been a hot topic in leadership and teamwork studies and books over the last 10-15 years. If we turn to the source of all rapidly changing knowledge, Wikipedia, we learn that "**Emotional intelligence** (EI) is the ability to monitor one's own and other people's **emotions**, to discriminate between different **emotions** and label them appropriately, and to use **emotional** information to guide thinking and behavior."

In a world of very open communicating in both professional and personal online settings, emotional intelligence continues to rise in importance as a personal attribute. Companies need to trust that their employees are speaking about their products and brands appropriately in public forums. They want to be able to trust that information will be shared through the proper channels and in their right context.

Emotionally intelligent coaches realize that they are not just being judged by the confidentiality they exhibit in working with their clients, but also in how they publicly interact with people that aren't their clients and may even be competitors. I've seen so many coaches that share questionable information on their Facebook and Twitter feeds that I'm surprised people are purchasing any coaching services from them at all. Sometimes they openly criticize clients or former partners in online forums. Anyone closely connected to them can easily figure out who they are referencing, but more importantly we start to wonder if they might do this to us at some point.

Follow the interactions the coach is having in online groups, on their own personal social pages, and personal websites/blogs. Over time you will see what they do and do not share, how they handle difficult online social interactions, and how others respond to their manner of communicating. Nowadays this is a very accessible way to find out about a future coach.

Emotional Intelligence Questions to Ponder

- How do they act in social networks?
- Do they contribute value? Do they just add to their own or do they contribute to others?
- Are they always selling? Is that acceptable with you?
- Are you proud to learn from them?
- Are they a shining example of what you want to become?

LET'S TALK MONEY

Price is what you pay. Value is what you get.
~ Warren Buffett

You have been waiting for this factor, haven't you? The money thing is interesting nowadays. We can get so much coaching for free! And, some of it is good! In fact, some of it is so good that we wonder why we should pay anyone at all for something that can be found free across the Internet.

The unfortunate truth is that we do often need to "put our money where our mouth is" and as a result we'll commit more to it. It isn't always the case, but how often do you collect "free" stuff and then save it to read, use, or consume later? Does later ever come? Perhaps. However, "later" often comes faster when we must put our hard-earned cash into something. There is an internal hope that we will "get our monies worth." If anything, we want to be able to confirm to ourselves that we didn't make a rash decision and purchase something that wasn't worth it.

Remember the $250 per month coaching package I purchased? The one where I saved all the homework and recordings on my computer until "later?" I didn't get as much out of it as I wanted to, but I was motivated to listen to ALL the sessions and read all the homework assignments at the end of the year because I had paid for them. I still have dozens of other freebies sitting in my computer that I haven't accessed because they were just too easy to obtain.

Did you know that many coaches are taught to increase their prices in their marketing training? They are taught that people value something that costs more than if it is free. So, by the sheer act of paying for their coaching services, the client will value the service more. This says a lot about human behavior. We often trick ourselves into believing we got our monies worth to prove to ourselves that we are smart decision makers and someone like ourselves would never make a rash or uninformed purchase. And, sometimes that may make a difference.

The Price is Right

What's the right price for a coach to charge for their services?

The answer is unfortunately the dreaded "it depends."

I used to make fun of this answer when I started managing programs and projects for the corporations I worked for in Washington, DC. Seriously, what kind of answer is that?

But it did depend? What was the experience of those performing the work? What were the unique limitations of certain projects – availability of people, travel time, expertise for a unique product development effort, number of other priorities being worked in parallel, politics, weather, etc.?

There were so many factors that determined if a project went well, stayed within the budget and schedule and ultimately succeeded in accomplishing the need it was expected to fill.

The same goes for coaching. The cost for services is first going to depend upon what the coach is charging. I've seen $20 an hour up to $500+ an hour. This is getting into prestigious law firm territory when we start looking at $500+ an hour rate.

Does a coach charging $500+ an hour have the same expertise as a seasoned lawyer who graduated from an Ivy League School?

Maybe and maybe not.

I wouldn't consider them overcharging if they are known for being excellent and experienced in their field. But, it is also important to remember that the high hourly rates some coaches may charge are purposefully set up to weed out the semi-serious client. Coaches value their time and money too. They often offer these higher coaching packages merely to ensure that they can maintain the time to fulfill other activities that bring in revenue and allow them to hone their skills. And, they are right to do so.

Securing a few high paying clients does ensure that they can ultimately be more focused and attentive to those that are paying them well. You also don't expect to be paying $500 an hour for 40 hours a week of coaching. These types of hourly rates are typically for one-time coaching sessions or for perhaps 1-2 a month brief phone calls, personal emails, a few online group sessions thrown in and heavy discounts to retreats and webinars. So, there are some extra perks for paying the higher prices.

Still, this might take a little time and effort on your part to sift through what is worth the price and what is not.

My pocketbook is lighter than in the past because I rushed into paying for some services too early without researching their free resources and references to find out if what the coach offered was truly right for me. Do you know what I do now? I purchase their book first.

After reading a book that resonated with me, I decided to check out the author online and found out that she was offering a course about how to create a course for about $250. The course spanned 2-3 months. I decided this was a good way to hone my course development skills AND get to know this coach a little better without paying too much. The course went well. Her corporate background was like mine. It seemed she resonated with all the clients even though we were from a variety of backgrounds. She was willing to share, not so wrapped up in sales, and had really built a community feeling in the group that she set up on Facebook.

Later in the year I noticed that she had a one-year coaching program that would take us through the basics of marketing. The program included two monthly conference calls, access to an online group, homework assignments and inclusion in a newsletter that she publishes on her website each year.
The cost of the program was $2500 for the year. Whew! That seems like a lot of money. However, I was confident that I would get the knowledge,

support and accountability that I needed through this program. I was not disappointed and am still connected to the people that I've met in that program and benefit from our connection.

Compare that to the program where I paid about the same to fly across the country to experience 3 days of "in-depth" training that was supposed to help me dig into the details of my business. It cost about the same, but I left feeling like it should have been free. We only scratched the surface of what was promised and during the 2-3 hours we were given to really roll up our sleeves and delve into our business, I was pulled aside and was drawn into a three hour up sell process for the high-end program.

It is important to pay people for the goods and services they offer. But, all goods and services are not created equal. Take advantage of all the free options (e.g. webinars, free downloads) and lower prices products (e.g. eBooks) that coaches offer.

Remember, you are accessing the free materials because you are on a recruiting mission to see if they are the right coach for you. I'm unwilling to pay $14.99 for a book written by a coach I've already paid $2,500.00 for coaching that didn't meet my needs, but I'm willing to give the same amount of money to a coach after reading their $10.99 book and realizing that the coach has something to offer that I need to grow.

Does that make sense?

Just because someone is high priced, does not mean they add more value. Most coaches are taught to offer a series of packages – a low, mid, and high-priced offering – so that you will choose the low or mid value offering. Yes, this helps clear out a lot of people, but this is one way they make additional money without individually coaching you.

Do you get exponentially more coaching if you get the high-priced package? Hopefully yes! However, depending upon your coaching need, you might not need the high touch that the highest package offers. You may have enough experience and expertise to go with the low to mid-range just to get your mind thinking of a few more options. Or, you may just need someone that focuses only on holding you accountable to goals you've already established.

This is a reminder that all these different factors work together toward ensuring you find the best coach for you. There are some great coaches out there that have a high-end package offering. Some of them have a great network of people surrounding them and purchasing the high-end package could be an opportunity to enter their inner circle of influencers and coaches. One high end coach might have a large following of entrepreneurs, but maybe a lot of them are in the beginning stages of business. However, there might be another high-end coach that just left a high-level position working for a highly respected organization. They demonstrate their connectedness to amazing people daily through their online interactions, who they interview, who they quote, etc. This may be someone worth paying more for because they are coming from an experience network of people that are confident in their success and are willing to ensure that other newcomers get to experience it as well.

You most likely care about money and so I left this factor toward the end of the book. It helps to get informed about the other factors first so that you can personally figure out which matter most and therefore inform your decisions on how much you are willing to pay to get what you want in a coaching relationship.

Money Questions to Ponder

- What free options does the coach make available so you can find out more about their knowledge and experience?
- How many coaching packages do they offer?
- Are there lower priced options that allow you to have some interaction with the coach toward informing larger purchasing decisions?
- Does their pricing include all the costs involved? For example, if you are attending a retreat, do they cover the food and sundries? Will you need to spend more to get a separate room?
- Do they offer different payment plans for high end services?

CRITERIA WORKSHEET

An inner process stands in need of outward criteria.
~ Ludwig Wittgenstein

Only you can determine who the best coach will be for you. Granted, it never hurts to get suggestions from friends or those you work with, but at the end of the day this is someone that is supposed to help you reach your next level of greatness. You get to determine what criteria are most important to you.

All the factors presented in this book are listed below. They are also accessible in a downloadable worksheet. But, for now look at this list and think about which of these factors are most important to you.

- Personal Values
- Experience
- Credentials and Formal Training
- Sources of Inspiration and Learning
- Personality
- Referrals
- Accountability Approach
- Administrative Approach

- Dependability
- Communication – Approach and tools
- Network
- Product Portfolio
- Time – commitment, time of day, time of life
- Confidentiality - The Human Vault
- Emotional Intelligence
- Money

Are you thinking what I'm thinking? All of these are important factors to consider. However, like the list my Dad had for purchasing the green wagon in 1980, there are some criteria that are more important.

The downloadable spreadsheet contains a formula or two embedded to make this a bit easier to calculate. You get to select, on a scale of 1-5, the importance level of each criterion. Then, you can rank order each coach you are considering according to each of the criteria.

The formulas are not "weighted," for those of you who are expecting that in the worksheet. It is important for you to visually see the priority you choose (in the 1st column of scores) as you compare your own scores.

Here's a screenshot of a sample worksheet with a few sample scores and comments filled in.

Criteria Worksheet

Factors and My Additional Criteria	My Priority Rating (1-5, 5 = highly important, must have)	Coach #1 Rating	Notes #1	Coach #2 Rating	Notes #2	Coach #3 Rating	Notes #3
Personal Values	5	5	Similar values	2	Some big differences that I think will impact relationship	3	Kind of similar values
Experience	4	3		2		2	
Credentials and Formal Training	2	2		2		1	
Sources of Inspiration and Learning	3	3		2		5	
Personality	3	3		2		5	
Referrals	3	3		1		5	
Accountability	3	3		5		5	
Administrative	3	4		3		4	
Dependability	3	3		3		3	
Communication	3	4		3		2	
Network	2	3		3		3	
Product Portfolio	1	3		2		2	
Time	3	4		3		2	
The Vault – confidentiality	5	2	Shares a bit much online	1		4	Good reference. Keeps private, private.
Emotional Intelligence	4	2		1		1	
Money (Cost)	1	1		1		1	
Add YOUR own here							
Totals	48	48		36		48	

Two of the coaches have the same exact score. However, one aligns closely with my values and the other falls a little lower on the scale. I have personally decided that I value that at a "5" and so even if two coaches have the same total score, I'll want to look to find out how closely each individual score mirrors what I told myself were my highest priorities.

You can always modify your personal scores as you come to recognize what you value most. But, doing so in a small table like this might help you in the process of figuring out where you are willing to settle for less and where you really want to make sure that you are staying focused on your real coaching needs. Coaching needs that you identified BEFORE you saw the slick website, the discounted coaching session, or the free downloadable worksheet.

You can download this excel worksheet at
http://nudgevillage.com/coach-factors.
The password is *coachfactors*.

I would highly recommend taking time to compare the factors and determine which are of the highest value for your needs. And, even adding extra weight/point values to those factors that are consistently important to you. That puts you in a strong position when you input data and determine the coach you should pursue.

Criteria Worksheet Questions to Ponder

- Do you know which criteria are most important to you?
- Do those criteria change depending upon the specific coaching need you are pursuing?
- Can you identify which criteria would be important for your coach to meet for any type of coaching you'd be seeking?
- Will you keep the criteria handy for those moments that you are making decisions and spending the money for a coach?

EXPERIMENT – MISTAKES AND LESSONS

> It's not an experiment if you know it's going to work.
> *~ Jeff Bezos*

You know what you need, at least some of what you need. You will only learn the rest of what is necessary for your success through constant experimenting and working with different people to reach your goals.

You will fall. You will give up. You will start to wonder if you've made the right decisions in selecting some of the coaches and mentors you work with. You may have reason to wonder. But, write those concerns and insights down. They will be invaluable when you seek out new coaches to enter new areas of expertise, pursue more difficult goals and run into new life challenges. Just keep pressing and know that every success, mistake and failure will arm you with the experience you need to make an even more informed decision the next time.

Might as well face it, you're addicted...

> Addiction isn't about substance - you aren't addicted to the substance, you are addicted to the alteration of mood that the substance brings.
> *~ Susan Cheever*

Some people get addicted to coaches and getting coached in general. There may be a time where you must stand back and perhaps consider a Coach Addiction Anonymous session.

I got caught in this rut a couple of years ago. I was so excited to be taking charge of my learning and growth that I signed up with multiple coaches. It was overwhelming! With some there were evening webinars, others had monthly assignments and still others have group coaching calls. It was too much for me. So much so that I was constantly consuming content, but not producing my own. I had to take a step back. I stepped back so far that I even added "Do not sign up with any coaches for the rest of this year" on my To Don't list just to make sure I was committed.

It's hard to say what the right balance is, but if you find yourself signing up for more coaching sessions than the time you spend on working on your goal, you may have found the personal tipping point. It is time to scale back a bit. You don't need to do what I did and wipe all coaches from your calendar. You may need to pare down your list or focus on one that will help you reach one of your most important goals. When that gets some traction, then it may be appropriate to re-engage with another coach for another goal.

A few suggestions if you are a coach addict:
- Find an accountability partner
- Join an online group to get community support
- Use mobile apps or electronic/offline tools to track your progress

OUTGROWING THE COACH

> Growth demands a temporary surrender of security.
> It may mean giving up familiar but limiting patterns, safe but unrewarding work, values no longer believed in, and relationships that have lost their meaning.
> ~ *John C. Maxwell*

You may outgrow your coach. This is especially true if you are getting started on simple goals and just needed a coach to get you going. Once you set the bar higher for yourself, you may find that you need to find a coach with more expertise, more connections, and more complex expectations. This is a wonderful place to be!

One of the problems in being at this point in growth is that we get comfortable. Though we initially took the risk to step out of our comfort zone and get a coach, we sometimes get so comfortable with them and our progress that we don't realize that it is time to move on and push ourselves into other zones of discomfort to ensure we continue to grow and progress.

As I shared earlier, the Entreleadership podcast (highly recommend) jolted me when the author made that statement about being in the wrong class if you were at the top of your class. I will admit to shedding a tear or two. Do I think that I'm the smartest person I know? Absolutely not. On the job, I'd become indispensable and that is great in many ways. But, the problem was that I was so indispensable in my role that the highest leadership levels couldn't imagine removing me from that role to allow me to move to the next level. They knew I could do it, but worried about what would happen if I moved on. Hearing this phrase in the podcast made me realize that I needed to be the person walking in the door learning from others so that I could grow to the next level. I quickly started making more time to train others in responsibilities that I needed to move on from and I was able to help them become indispensable in their roles.

I also knew it was time for me to pursue other opportunities for my growth and learning and close out that phase of contributing in that organization. Try as they might to provide further growth opportunities for me (and they did do that), they encountered constraints that prevented them from creating new positions. Ironically, a position did open that looked good on paper, but I knew that it wouldn't provide the growth I needed to progress to the next level. So, I was able to turn it down in favor of looking for "the right class" for me.

You will grow and progress. You will get close to some of those that coach you. Yet, there will be a time to let go and move forward to the next phase of your growth. It may be toward more expertise; it may be in a different direction. Whatever the reason, continue to be open, as you were when you went out on a limb to select your first coach, to keep pursuing those that can help you get into the "right class" for you.

There is a quote that I remember from my youth. "Make new friends but keep the old. One is silver, and the other is gold." Stay in touch with your old coaches. You may become a great person to refer others to them and they will appreciate the business. You may also work together on a project or in a networking environment at some point. They could become your biggest advocate as you get your book written, your business started, or whatever next big step you plan to take. You may even become accountability partners at some point instead of maintaining a coaching relationship. In whatever case, maintain the relationship. Both of you will benefit.

NOW, GO – FIND THE PERFECT COACH FOR YOU

Coach's voice will never leave my head as long as I live.

~ Allen Iverson

Do you feel ready to go find the perfect coach for you? I hope there were at least one or two key thoughts or points that you can take with you into your next search for a coach. I'm sure that you or other readers will have a few tips of your own to add. I'd love to hear them so that each new version of this book becomes more helpful to the next reader. Feel free to share them with me through one of my social networks.

We all have our preferences and I'm certainly not exempt. But, I encourage you to take a step back before you make your next decision and reflect for at least a few minutes on the factors presented in this book.

Now get out there and find a coach to help you achieve your next goal. I'm confident the right coach is out there preparing to help you go to the next level of personal growth.

Good luck!

BOOKS

A Sequence of Little Nudges
Find Your Ideal Accountability Partner
Find the Perfect Coach for You
The Nudge Factor: Wielding Influence in Our Human Orbits

ABOUT THE AUTHOR

Rebecca Clark works in the training and development field. She is an intrapreneur, entrepreneur, and a curator of life experiences. Other books include *A Sequence of Little Nudges, The Nudge Factor: Wielding Influence in Our Precise Human Orbits* and *Find Your Ideal Accountability Partner.* She also develops online courses on similar topics.

She currently resides in the Washington, DC area.

www.ingramcontent.com/pod-product-compliance
Lightning Source LLC
Chambersburg PA
CBHW030712220526
45463CB00005B/2012